T

No one can serve two masters, for either he will hate the one and love the other, or he will be devoted to the one and despise the other. Matthew 6:24

By Fay Velez

Dedicated to all those who have been affected by Freemasonry: bringing freedom and enlightenment to open their eyes to the truth and for that truth to bring freedom.

...if the Son makes you free,
you shall be free indeed.
John 8:36

Published 2024

TABLE OF CONTENTS

Table of Contents

INTRODUCTION

I am writing this from the viewpoint of what I have seen personally regarding Freemasonry. I do not claim to be an expert in the knowledge of Freemasonry. But being a deliverance minister, I have seen so many people bound up with demonic strongholds that keep them from having a normal life. I have seen people that have disassociated themselves from the world due to the damage that was done to them due to their parents and grandparents being in the Masons. I have seen people that have dealt with all kinds of infirmities in their lives and that same infirmity go down to their children because the generational curse of Freemasonry had not been cut off of them and their bloodline.

My prayer is that this book will help you to identify the spirits, and infirmities that are still attached to you due to Freemasonry still being in your bloodline.

This book will open your eyes to some keys to use to get free from the stronghold of Freemasonry that has kept you bound for so many years.

This book leads you in a prayer to pray to bring freedom to you and your family from the demonic stronghold that Freemasonry can have on you.

This book teaches you about what Freemasonry is, and the lies and deception that it uses to progressively draw you in. It talks about why Christians should not be a Mason.

My prayer is that as you read this book that it will open your eyes to the truth about Freemasonry. My prayer is as you learn the truth, you will ask God to set you free from all involvement with it, knowingly or unknowingly, so that you can walk in freedom.

About the Author:

Fay Velez is an ordained Christian International (CI) Minister. Her and her husband Tom lead the Prophetic Healing and Deliverance Ministry at Vision Church at the Christian International Headquarters (VCCI) in Santa Rosa Beach, Florida. They also lead the 8:30am daily morning prayer meeting Monday – Friday, and the 7pm VCCI communion service, live on Monday nights.

They are also on the Prophetic team and have a traveling ministry.

Fay is on staff at Christian International as the Director of the Vision Investment Partner program.

Fay holds a Biblical degree from CI, and functions in the fivefold ministry office of a Prophet. She is especially gifted in the discerning of spirits, deliverance, prophecy, prophetic counseling, spiritual warfare, healing, and intercession.

Fay and her husband Tom have been teaching and ministering on prayer, the gifts of the Holy Spirit, prophesying over individuals, doing personal deliverance, and administering the Lord's healing through the wonderful name of Jesus Christ for over 30 years.

They have both led many to Jesus and have led many into the Baptism of the Holy Spirit with the evidence of speaking in tongues.

CHAPTER 1 What is Freemasonry

Freemasonry is an open door for many to have demons. A lot of people have demons because of them or someone in their family line being in the Masons.

Freemasonry is a blend of occult, paganism, satanism, demonology, and spiritualism.

In Freemasonry the one true God (our God) has been replaced by a false god. It is identified in the Masonic lodge as the Grand Architect or Great Architect of the Universe.

John 14:11 and 13 tells believers to call upon the God the Father in the name of Jesus. In the Masonic lodge prayers are directed to the Grand Architect of the Universe.

Masons deliberately omit the holy name of Jesus Christ from their prayers. They teach that good works alone is your guarantee to Heaven, with no need for Jesus.

Masons do not worship the Christian God Jesus. They worship a generic Grand Architect of the Universe.

The goal of the Masons has always been to change America from a Christian nation into a secular society. They appear to be just good ole boys that do good works.

Most people do not learn the truth about the Masons until entering the higher degrees. But the truth is Masons lie and deceive, just like Satan. Just as Satan comes deceptively like an angel of Light, the Masons also try to appear as angels of Light and goodness.

Mason converts are lied to in their lower degrees of membership.

Satan and higher degree Masons have much the same goals. That is to deceive people. They deceive people by wanting to help those in need. That way, they are perceived as good people, and that assistance, or charity, brings a debt of gratitude from the receiver. Satan even comes to us as an angel of light, deceiving many, just as the Masons do. The Masons are a society of secrets and deceptions.

One of my family member's husband was in the Masons. When it started it seemed so innocent. Their son was born with breathing issues. They needed this expensive machine, and they had no insurance. The Masons stepped in and really helped them. This opened the door for my family member's husband to be sucked into the plan of Satan as he continued to go deeper and deeper into the Masons. Each level was a greater responsibility and more vows and more things that had to be kept secret.

Masons repeatedly go to different religions for direction. Almost none of the Masons teaching comes from Christianity, what small amount that does, is twisted.

These different religions string you along and finally tell you there is no God, and that you are a god because you are following their teaching. These teachings are greedy and selfish. They teach you it is okay if it is helping you to get ahead to win at any cost, even if you have to lie and cheat to get to your goal.

These teachings tell you to follow the Masonic path and you will be successful. They tell you there is no hell, that there is no higher authority than Lucifer.

Once people get to the higher degrees and they believe the Masonic lies, it is hard for them to let go. They have made so many vows and they have been sworn to secrecy. Then, they start realizing the Grand Architect of the Universe is not the God of the Old Testament.

As they continue to follow the Masonic path, they will shed layers from their old religion. They will also shed their loyalties outside of the Masons.

This will conceal their own personal true identity. This will also isolate them from others and keep them from seeing the only true God. It is like they have blindfolds on and they cannot see the truth.

The secret of Masonry is that you will be tricked into believing there is useful knowledge to be learned in the Masons. This knowledge will be costly and time-consuming.

It will require a lot of time away from your family. You will be made to swear things taking solemn oaths. After a while you have chosen the lodge, the occult, and Satan over the Lord Jesus Christ.

By the time you see that the mention of Jesus has been blotted out, you will feel trapped because of all the solemn Masonic oaths you have made without knowing in advance of just what you were in for. You will already have sworn to keep all oaths secret or the penalty is death.

CHAPTER 2 Difference between Freemasonry and Christianity.

The main difference between Freemasonry and Christianity is that Christianity holds that Jesus is everything. Masons teach that Jesus is nothing. That He is equal to pagan gods. In the Masons, Jesus is not mentioned. Prayers are not said in the name of Jesus. When scriptures are quoted, they leave out the name of Jesus.

Christianity rejects all false gods. They only worship the true God, the God of the Bible. They should have no part in any type of ritual that honors pagan gods.

Exodus 20:4 says, you shall not make for yourself an idol in the form of anything in heaven above or on the earth beneath or in the waters below.

This is one of the Ten Commandments that Moses received from the hand of God and brought down from the mountain.

Deuteronomy 7:25 says, the images of their gods you are to burn in the fire. Do not covet the silver and gold on them, and do not take it for yourselves, or you will be ensnared by it, for it is detestable to the LORD your God.

Deuteronomy 11:16 says, be careful, or you will be enticed to turn away and worship other gods and bow down to them.

Psalms 81:9 says, you shall have no foreign god among you; you shall not worship any god other than me.

Isaiah 42:8 says, I am the Lord; that is my name! I will not give my glory to another or my praise to idols.

1 John 5:21 says, Dear children, keep yourselves from idols.

The Bible warns us about taking excessive oaths. Christians should let their yes be yes and their no be no. Any oath they do take, they need to take it seriously and it needs to line up with the word of God.

The Bible teaches that Jesus is special and that He is not just one Messiah among many, but He is the only Messiah.

Christians believe that there is only one God. Yet, the one God is three distinct Persons. God the Father, God the Son, and God the Holy Spirit. These three have distinct personal attributes, but there is no division.

Christians believe they are saved by grace that comes through faith in Jesus Christ.

Titus 3:5 says, He saved us, not because of righteous things we have done, but because of his mercy. He saved us through the washing of rebirth and renewal by the Holy Spirit.

Christians believe that personal faith in Jesus is the only way to be saved. They believe Jesus is the way, the truth, and the life. They believe those who have a personal relationship with Jesus, have eternal life with Him.

Freemasonry believes in all gods. They have many rituals that contain excessive oaths. Their teachings contain pagan and occultic teachings. They omit the name of Jesus in all they do. They twist Christianity teachings and omit the name of Jesus.

Freemasonry teaches that salvation depends on good works. The Worshipful Master is a symbol of the Redeemer to them. They deny that faith in Jesus is the only way of salvation.

Freemasonry does not care who you worship. You can worship any god or any religion, they do not care. They belief that no religion can claim to be superior to another. They believe that whatever someone believes is truth to them and the Masons are okay with that.

Freemasonry is not a Godly religion. Many, if not most, members believe in the Grand Architect of the Universe. They are all about work and charities, making themselves look good. They want people to believe that they are an organization of people who believe in helping others. But there are so many hidden things that are not revealed until you become a higher level in the Masons.

Masons never end a prayer in the name of Jesus. They end it by saying "so mote it be". This is a ritual phrase that they use meaning "so may it be".

Christianity and Freemasonry are opposite of each other. Christianity believes that the only way to heaven is by Jesus Christ. Christianity believes in the word of God and following the word of God. They pray in the name of Jesus.

Freemasonry believes you get to heaven by works. They twist the scriptures, and they never pray in the name of Jesus. I believe as a believer in Jesus Christ that you should not join the Masons and that you should not be a part of them in any way.

CHAPTER 3 Open doors to the demonic

God's word tells us that His people perish for lack of knowledge.

Hosea 4:6 says, my people are destroyed from lack of knowledge. Because you have rejected knowledge, I also will reject you from being priest for me; Because you have forgotten the law of your God, I also will forget your children.

This verse is telling us that we are being destroyed because we do not know God.

When we are involved in the Masons, and we participate in their rituals, it opens the doors for the demonic to put diseases and infirmities on us.

I believe it opens the door for the leviathan spirit to come to us and to our family. This spirit wraps around a person's spine, and twists it, causing scoliosis, back pain, neck tightness, insomnia. It makes you get sleepy when you are reading or studying God's word. It opens the door for fibromyalgia and cancer. It causes headaches.

A lot of times the leviathan spirit enters through emotional wounds from our parents. It also can enter if someone in your bloodline was involved in the Freemasons due to a curse that comes down through the blood line because of things done in secret.

The Freemasons pledge secret oaths to Allah and against Christianity. They worship Lucifer, or Satan. The symbol they have chosen to represent their god is the All-Seeing Eye, which the Egyptians used to represent their pagan god.

The Masons teach a false plan of salvation. They are not following in the teaching of Jesus Christ.

2 John 1:9 says "Whoever transgresses and does not abide in the doctrine of Christ does not have God. He who abides in the doctrine of Christ has both the Father and the Son."

They are classic paganism.

1 Corinthians 10:20-21 says, rather, that the things which the Gentiles sacrifice they sacrifice to demons and not to God, and I do not want you to have fellowship with demons. You cannot drink the cup of the Lord and the cup of demons; you cannot partake of the Lord's Table and of the table of demons."

This verse tells us that the sacrifices of pagans are offered to demons, rather than God. The Freemasons always refer to the Grand Architect of the Universe instead of Jesus Christ.

When our ancestors have been a Grandmaster of a lodge or if they dealt in witchcraft, the leviathan spirit can increase in a greater level into our lives.

If you have continuous anxiety and neck or back pain these are signs that you may have a leviathan spirit.

Leviathan is a demonic spirit that has pride. It is a critical spirit, causing confusion, impatience, a lying tongue, and discord. It also attempts to twist the meaning of words spoken, to cause misunderstanding, offence, etc.

These are reflected in Proverbs 6:16-19: "These six things the Lord hates, Yes, seven are an abomination to Him: A proud look, A lying tongue, Hands that shed innocent blood, A heart that devises wicked plans, Feet that are swift in running to evil, A false witness who speaks lies, and one who sows discord among brethren."

My husband and I head up the deliverance ministry at our church in Santa Rosa Beach, FL. We have seen while doing deliverance, that many people who deal with sinus issues have a history of Masonic involvement by either themselves, their spouse, or their ancestors.

We have seen time and time again when we are ministering deliverance to someone, and they seem to not be able to get rid of an infirmity, that it was tied to Masonic involvement. When we cut the Freemasonry connection off of them. They are able to receive their healing.

CHAPTER 4 Devil having a legal right to attack

When we do deliverance, we normally have to deal with tearing down strongholds, which can involve removing legal rights and casting the demonic influences out. We cannot cast a demon out if it has a legal right to be there.

What are legal rights and how does it work? It is when a demon has a legal right to remain in our life and harass us, due to the legal right not being cut off.

The demonic can have a legal right to continue to attack us if we have willful sin in our life. I believe the bigger the sin the wider the door can be opened. Sin opens the door to demons, and this pushes us into more sin.

Negative soul ties can also give the devil a legal right to attack us. Having sex out of marriage or committing adultery opens the door to the demonic. This creates a negative soul tie that is like a hose pipe between two people that demons can use to their advantage to pass from one person to another. If the person you had sex with had demons tormenting them, it unites the two of you together and then the devil has a legal right to torment both of you.

Negative soul ties do not just have to be formed by sex outside of marriage. They can be created through unhealthy relationships. Making an ungodly vow or having a piece of jewel that was given to you when you were in an adulterous relationship can cause a negative soul tie.

Ungodly vows can be like a spiritual agreement that the enemy uses as a legal right to gain access into your life. When someone joins a cult a lot of times they are required to make vows with the devil.

Reading horoscopes can give the enemy your spiritual agreement. When you read horoscopes, it tells the enemy that you are interested in the things of the demonic. Jesus warns us about making vows.

Unforgiveness is another way the enemy can have a legal right to torment us. God will not forgive us, if we do not forgive others. I have heard that the most common reason that people are not healed is due to unforgiveness in their heart, and ancestral sins. When you involve yourself in the occult world, and I believe that Freemasonry is in this category, you not only open demonic doors in your life, but you also open it in the lives of your children and grandchildren.

Exodus 20:5 says, you must not bow down to them or worship them, for, I the Lord your God, am a jealous God who will not tolerate your affection for any other gods. I lay the sins of the parents upon their children; the entire family is affected, even children in the third and fourth generations of those who reject me.

If your ancestors have committed sin or if they have been in the occult, ask God for forgiveness. Even though you are not personally guilty of those sins, they may have caused curses in your life. Those curses need to be cut off and broken from your life, because you may be in the second, third, or fourth generation of someone that was guilty of this.

In the Masons they speak a lot of self-curses over themselves. They do this by worshiping the Grand Architect, omitting the name of Jesus when they pray, twisting the scriptures so they are not true.

When you are in the Mason and you participate in this, you are speaking word curses over yourself, and you are cursing yourself.

The Masons give you aprons and rings. These things have a demon attached to them. As long as you hang on to these things, and as long as you have not cut the demonic strongholds that were attached to you from them, the devil still has a legal right to torment you.

The way you get released from the strongholds is to verbally confess and repent of your sins that have given the enemy legal right to attack you.

1 John 1:9 tells us to confess our sins. If we don't confess our sins and instead, we hide them from God, it leaves that sin remaining in our lives. We need to confess our sins in order to be forgiven.

Below is a prayer you can pray to break and cut off any or all of the connections you have had with these demonic strongholds.

Prayer:
Jesus, I come to You today and I repent for all sins in my life, and I ask You to forgive me. In Jesus' name, I cut off all negative soul ties and I command them to go back to the people they belong to and never enter me again. I ask You Lord to forgive me for any demonic vows I have made, and I release them to You today in Jesus' name. Lord, I ask You to set me free from any unforgiveness in my heart. I repent for holding any bitterness in my heart toward others and I forgive everyone that has hurt me, in Jesus' name. Lord, I repent for any involvement that I have had in the Masons and any ancestral sins, I ask You to cut off any legal ground where the

enemy has had a legal right to torment me, in Jesus' name. In Jesus' name, I cancel every curse that I have written or spoken over myself, and I call it void in my life. Lord, I repent for taking any objects that were not Godly and in Jesus' name, I cut off any demonic attachment that is still attacked to these objects. Lord, I receive my freedom today and I thank You that who the Son sets free is free indeed, in Jesus' name. Amen

CHAPTER 5 Lies and Deceptions

Lies and covering up is expected of Masons. Even if they go to trial, they have to keep their obligations to the Mason's and cover up or lie, even if they know the truth.

When you go to your first meeting of the Masons, they want you to think that they are a group of men who are in darkness and are searching for the light, just a group of good ole boys. That is a lie, and it is deceptive. The main focus of the Masons is all based on lies and deceptions. As you go deeper into the different levels you will see that it just gets darker and darker.

The Masons do not look at Jesus as the savior. They do not use the name of Jesus. But they hide all this at the beginning. But, quickly you are drawn into their world. This world is filled with secrets, lies, deception and cover ups.

The Masons have many secret words, handshakes, signals, etc. They use some Bible names and verses, but they twist them to fit their ritual. Everyone that joins the Masons has to declare their faith in a Supreme Being before they can be initiated. This Supreme Being is not the God we serve, it is the Grand Architect of the Universe.

When you are in the Masonic lodge you cannot call on Jehovah God, you always are talking to the Grand Architect of the Universe.

Exodus 20:3 says, you shall have no other gods before me.

Psa. 81:9 says, you shall have no foreign god among you; you shall not bow down to an alien god.

Deception can be defined:

- As the act of causing someone to accept as true or valid what is false or invalid.
- The act of deceiving.
- To mislead by giving a distorted impression or false sense of reality.
- To trick or to cheat.

- Trusting false promises or believing a lie.

Freemasonry binds the people that are involved in the Masons to be true to each other, even while it lies to them in the innermost secrets. Freemasonry is full of lies and deceptions, but the people do not realize this until later on. In the beginning everything looks good.

Freemasons are not completely open about their membership. Like I said earlier, they hide a lot of the things that happen before they get you hooked. You are not allowed to discuss things that happen in the lodge room in great detail. It is full of secrets, lies, deception and cover ups.

CHAPTER 6 What does the Bible say about Freemasonry

The Bible does not address the Masonic by name, but it does give us a framework to access the beliefs of Freemasonry. Masonic practices do not agree with biblical teachings.

When you research Freemasonry, one main issue is their demands for secrecy in their oaths and allegiance. The Bible shares a life of honor, being real and an unwavering devotion to God. This is one of the areas that Christians question about Freemasonry. The secretive oaths, and allegiances within Freemasonry go against what the Bible says regarding Christians serving God openly and without doubt.

Freemasonry does not share openly about Jesus. God and Jesus are not even mentioned in their prayers. They tell people you get to heaven by your works, not by believing in Jesus as your Lord and Savior.

The word of God tells us not to be unequal yoked, but Freemasonry welcomes all members. They do not care if they are Hindu or Budda or whatever, because they do not focus on God.

Below are some scriptures that will help you understand why you should not participate in Freemasonry.

Matthew 5:33-37 Again, you have heard that it was said to the people long ago, 'Do not break your oath, but fulfill to the Lord the vows you have made. But I tell you, do not swear an oath at all: either by heaven, for it is God's throne; or by the earth, for it is his footstool; or by Jerusalem, for it is the city of the Great King. And do not swear by your head, for you cannot make even one hair white or black. All you need to say is simply 'Yes' or 'No'; anything beyond this comes from the evil one.[a]

2 Corinthians 6:14-17 Do not be yoked together with unbelievers. For what do righteousness and wickedness have in common? Or what fellowship can light have with darkness? What harmony is there between Christ and Belial? Or what does a believer have in common with an unbeliever? What agreement is there between the temple of God and idols? For we are the temple of the living God. As God has said: "I will live with them and walk among them, and I will be their God, and they will be my people. "Therefore, "Come out from them and be separate, says the Lord. Touch no unclean thing, and I will receive you."

Ephesians 5:11-12 Put on the full armor of God, so that you can take your stand against the devil's schemes. For our struggle is not against flesh and blood, but against the rulers, against the authorities, against the powers of this dark world and against the spiritual forces of evil in the heavenly realms.

James 5:12 Above all, my brothers, and sisters, do not swear—not by heaven or by earth or by anything else. All you need to say is a simple "Yes" or "No." Otherwise you will be condemned.

1 Corinthians 10:21-22 You cannot drink the cup of the Lord and the cup of demons too; you cannot have a part in both the Lord's table and the table of demons. Are we trying to arouse the Lord's jealousy? Are we stronger than he?

Acts 4:12 Salvation is found in no one else, for there is no other name under heaven given to mankind by which we must be saved."

1 John 1:6-7 If we claim to have fellowship with him and yet walk in the darkness, we lie and do not live out the truth. But if we walk in the light, as he is in the light, we have fellowship with one another, and the blood of Jesus, his Son, purifies us from all sin.

2 Timothy 3:16-17 All Scripture is inspired by God and is useful to teach us what is true and to make us realize what is wrong in our lives. It corrects us when we are wrong and teaches us to do what is right. God uses it to prepare and equip his people to do every good work.

Revelation 2:20 Nevertheless, I have this against you: You tolerate that woman Jezebel, who calls herself a prophet. By her teaching she misleads my servants into sexual immorality and the eating of food sacrificed to idols.

Colossians 2:8 See to it that no one takes you captive through hollow and deceptive philosophy, which depends on human tradition and the elemental spiritual forces of this world rather than on Christ.

Know that the Masons' main focus is to not worship God, but a Supreme Being. (The Grand Architect)

Things Freemasonry does that the Bible does not agree with:

- They swear secret oaths.

The Bible does not allow Christian to take these kind of oaths.

Matthew 5:34-37 But I tell you, do not swear an oath at all either by heaven, for it is God's throne; or by the earth, for it is his footstool; or by Jerusalem, for it is the city of the Great King. And do not swear by your head, for you cannot make even one hair white or black. All you need to say is simply Yes or No, anything beyond this comes from the evil one.

- They practice idolatry.

The Bible teaches that idolatry is a sin, and that God hates it, this is the first two commandments.

- They teach Universalism.

Freemasonry teaches that all religious paths lead to the same God. They worship The Great Architect of the Universe. They do not worship Our God and they do not acknowledge him as the Holy Trinity: the Father, Son, and Holy Spirit. They assign him a generic name that is fitting for any of their members.

- They claim difficult secrets.

Jesus taught that all of His teachings were made known to everyone nothing was kept secret.

John 18:20 I have spoken openly to the world," Jesus replied. "I always taught in synagogues or at the temple, where all the

Jews come together. I said nothing in secret.

- They teach works are righteousness.

They believe their works give them favor in the eyes of whatever God they choose to worship.

Ephesians 2:8-9 says, for by grace you have been saved through faith. And this is not your own doing; it is the gift of God, not a result of works, so that no one may boast.

So, my belief as a believer with all that the Bible has to say, we should not have any part of the Masons.

CHAPTER 7 Demonic strongholds Freemasonry has on believers.

What is a stronghold? It is a faulty thinking pattern based on lies and deceptions. One of the devil's main weapons is deception. Deception is a building block for strongholds. Strongholds blind our eyes and keep us from hearing so that we do not receive God's best.

A good example of a stronghold could be you are afraid of God, and you have a hard time feeling His love and presence. You see Him as someone that will hurt you. So, you put up a wall. This wall makes it hard for you to receive God's love, presence, and joy, and it keeps you from drawing close to Him.

It is so important to have the right perception of God if we want to live a victorious life.

Freemasonry has demonic strongholds on people that have joined their society, or people that are in the blood line of people who have joined their society. Due to the lies and deception that they portray, it opens the door for the demonic to connect or create strongholds in our lives. Strongholds may be infirmity, financial problems, divorce, robbery and so much more. We have to cut off the strongholds.

2 Corinthians 10:4 says, for the weapons of our warfare are not carnal, but mighty through God to the pulling down of stronghold.

Strongholds are birthed in deception. These are lies and false beliefs. We have to bring the truth of God's word to these strongholds.

We need to know that our primary offensive weapon is the sword of the Spirit, which is the word of God.

Eph. 6:17 says, the sword of the Spirit is the word of God.

The word of God causes deception and lies to vanish. So, the more truth we bring into the situation, the more darkness will flee. We have to know God's word, so we know the power of His word to tear down the strongholds that have kept us in bondage.

John 8:31-36 Jesus tells us that we can be held in bondage due to strongholds in our lives. And His solution was for us to continue in His word, and we shall know the truth, and the truth shall make us free.

2 Corinthians 10:4 tells us, the weapons we fight with are not the weapons of the world. On the contrary, they have divine power to destroy strongholds.

So how can these demonic strongholds be overcome? First, we need to use the right weapon. Paul tells us in 2 Corinthians 10:3 for though we walk in the flesh, we are not waging war according to the flesh. We do not use human weapons; We as believers should depend on the power of God's word and the name of Jesus, to overcome the powers of evil.

Knowing the truth and the power of God's word, with the name of Jesus, we can destroy all the arguments and deceptions against the knowledge of God.

When we depend on God, we can deal with these arguments and deceptions, because we know the truth. We can have authority over them with the power of Jesus in us, and we can stand against them when they occur.

Regarding Freemasonry, we have to cut off the lies and deceptions, and destroy false ideas and arguments that have been used against us.

The truth of God's word gives us a clear foundation that lets us know right from wrong. We need to use God's word to go after the demonic strongholds in our life and to be set free of them. Then we will be able to see the lies and deceptions that have covered things up. We will be able to see into the demonic realm, and see the plans and strategies of the enemy, which has been sent against us, due to us or our ancestors being a part of the Masons.

We as believers have to stand against the wickedness that has come against us and cut it off of our lives. We need to repent if we had anything to do with partnering with this sin, knowingly or unknowingly.

Satan has no defense against the Word of God, and the word of God is our weapon against Satan.

Freemasonry has a lot of deception in their lodges. We have to know that the word of God is our defense against the attacks of the enemy and where he tried to gain a foothold.

Even if we never had anything to do with Freemasonry but it has come down our blood line, we still have to cut it off. We have to come against the demonic strongholds that have had a legal right to attack us, due to the connection with the Masons not having been cut off of us.

If you do not know the word of God, or you do not understand it, you have a disadvantage when Satan comes after you.

So, you have to read and study God's word, and you have to be ready at all times.

As believers, we need to destroy Satan's strongholds in our lives. We do this by destroying every evil thought, and anything that rises up against the word of God and come into agreement with the word of God.

In other words, we need to command any thought, any habit, any behavior, any experience, and anything that is not obeying Christ in our lives, to be destroyed, and come into agreement with Christ's authority. If we do, we resist the devil, he will flee. (Psalm, 44:5 & 18:39)

Jesus commanded Satan to be gone and Satan left. We have that same authority, and no stronghold, no matter how long it has been built, can withstand the power of the name of Jesus.

Our battles are not in this world. Our weapons are not physical. Our warfare is spiritual. Our weapons are those of the full armor of God. They consist of the belt of truth buckled around our waist, with the breastplate of righteousness in place, and with our feet fitted with the readiness that comes from knowing the gospel of peace. We also need to take up the shield of faith, with which we can resist all the attacks of the evil one. Take the helmet of salvation, which is our thought life and attitude, and the sword of the Spirit, which is the word of God. (Ephesians 6:14-17)

Know that our power comes from God and His plan is to destroy spiritual strongholds.

CHAPTER 8 Negative effects of Freemasonry

If you are a Mason and you become a Christian, it leaves you in a difficult position with the lodge. The lodge considers Christians as being unworthy to receive the Light. When the Masons speak of the Light, they are referring to a Supreme Being (The Grand Architect of the Universe) not the God of the Bible we serve.

When a person joins the Masons during the ceremony of initiation, the person is required to undertake an obligation, swearing on the religious volume sacred to his personal faith.

The greatest problem for a Christian Mason is that by taking the oaths of the Craft (Freemasonry), and living his life according to them, he has opened the door to Lucifer to steal his relationship with the living God.

Freemasonry purposefully makes the status of Jesus Christ and the Holy Spirit become less. They are placed below God the Father, disallowing the triune nature of the biblical God.

Freemasonry has many mysteries which have their roots in other religions, of the world that brought on the wrath of the Hebrew God of the Old Testament. The Masons deceive the people, and they do not know what is really going on until they are at a much higher level. They deliberately lead people astray, and they are all about vows and secrets.

For example, the letter G. A Christian would interpret the symbol as God, whereas the pagan would see it as knowledge or gnosis. Gnosis in the Masons is attaining secret knowledge, and this is the way they find their salvation, and overcome the material world. People are misled by false interpretations.

The Masons do not want people to understand them. Their deceptions are intentional.

One of the damages of being a Mason is that you may be a part of the lodge thinking it is an extension of your Christian faith, when in fact it very well may be a trojan horse, allowing another god in your soul.

The god of Freemasonry, and the God of the Bible are not one and the same. There is a great difference between the two. The Masonic god, the Great Architect of the Universe is believed to be above all other gods. The Masonic god is all-inclusive and all-embracing.

The biblical God is lowered to the level of all the other gods. It is also rendered as equal with the false gods of those religions. So, Christianity is stripped of its uniqueness as the one true religion that offers humanity its only hope for salvation.

The god of Freemasonry is believed by some in the lodge to be the God of the Bible. But they soon find out this is not true. Because this god is not the triune God of the Christian faith.

The Masonic god is given a greater position among all other gods. This god is single in nature and not the triune God of the Bible. This god is a force, it is a principle.

In the Masons, Jesus Christ is not one with the Father, and He is not looked to for salvation.

Luke 4:8 says, it is written, you shall worship the Lord your God and serve Him only.

Deut. 6:13-15 says, "you shall fear only the Lord your God; and you shall worship Him . . . you shall not follow other gods, any of the gods of the peoples who surround you, for the Lord your God in the midst of you is a jealous God; otherwise the anger of the Lord your God will be kindled against you, and He will wipe you off the face of the earth.

So, I really believe that you cannot be a Christian and continue to be a Mason too. You have to choose who you will serve the God of the Bible, or the god of Freemasonry.

The Masons are greatly influenced by the occult. They say that Jesus was just a man. Jesus Christ was not accepted as the one who saves us and gives us eternal life. Again, the lodge does not allow the name of Jesus to be mentioned in any of their prayers or rituals. The lodge has rewritten scriptures for their benefit.

Deuteronomy 4:2 say, you shall not add to the work which I am commanding you, nor take away from it.

It does not please God that the lodge has taken scripture and changed it to make it say what they want it to say. All prayers are directed to the Grand Architect of the Universe.

God says in His word that everyone therefore who shall confess Me before me, I will also confess him before My Father who is in heaven. But whoever shall deny Me before men, I will also deny him before My Father who is in heaven,

So, the Bible is clear about what Jesus said regarding those who are ashamed of His Son. Jesus does not take it lightly regarding the Masons taking His place of reverence and worship.

The Masons deliberately keep their secrets from the people in the lodge. They use false explanations and misinterpretations of its symbols to mislead the people, and to keep the truth from them.

The lodge speaks of Lucifer (Satan) as the light-bearer. Lucifer, the son of the morning. They say it is Lucifer who bears the light. Masonry claims to be the light that awakens our minds to his perfection and ultimate divinity. Again, you cannot serve the lodge and God. You have to choose.

There is so much secrecy in Freemasonry. They intentionally keep you in the dark, so you do not know the truth. They make you swear oaths, and these oaths have penalties to them. These penalties are to cause fear, obedience, and terror in you.

Our God, the real true God, is not a God of fear and misery. He is a God of mercy, love, and compassion.

The Masons loyalty is not to the God of Christianity, but to all gods. The people that are in the Masons really believe that the penalties that come with these oaths will be carried out. There is a lot of fear when you are in the Masons.

The Masons do not see the Bible as being inspired by God. They only see it as a symbol of divine will, law, or revelation. The Masons omitted the reference in the Bible regarding salvation and wrote it in a way that would not offend anyone of another religion. They look to themselves for purification not the God of the Bible.

The Masons do not accept that man is born sinful and that they are in need of redemption.

Many Christians believe once a Mason, always a Mason. They have a hard time seeing the difference between the teaching of the Church, and that of the lodge. I feel there is a demonic stronghold on them, that tries to keep them from seeing the true light.

It seems that even if they are able to see the truth, and leave the lodge, they are unable to mentally sever the tie that bound them to the lodge. They feel the tug: "Once a Mason, always a Mason. This is a lie from hell. It is probably negative soul ties that are still connected that have not been cut off. They need to be cut off, with the name of Jesus Christ.

Again, it is impossible to serve two masters' without loving one and despising the other.

CHAPTER 9 How to be set free from Freemasonry

Many people have been involved in Freemasonry. Either they have been directly involved or someone in their blood line has been in Freemasonry. In either case, they need to be set free from the strongholds they have on their lives.

Most Christians have been against Masonry because they do not believe in taking oaths of secrecy. These oaths come with threats of evil and even death if you share them. There is a lot of fear, even up to the 33rd degree.

There are a lot of physical and emotional issues that have happened to people due to personal or ancestral involvement in the Masons. These include conditions such as depression, multiple personality disorders, heart issues, post-traumatic stress disorder, suicide tendencies, migraine headaches, bleeding ulcer, homosexuality and so much more.

When you are your family have been in the Masons there is an over-abundance of health issues.

The Masons are filled with secrecy and curses. They contain no spiritual truth. These secrecy and curses only serve to hide, deceive, and confuse those who are in the Masons. Masonry takes selected pieces of Christianity and puts them on top of anti-Christian foundations.

If you or your ancestors participated in Freemasonry, you need to have a spiritual cleansing and pray a prayer of deliverance over yourself. Involvement in Freemasonry results in spiritual bondage for you and your family line.

Like I said earlier, most Masons are unaware of the false theology, pagan mysticism and occultism that undergirds the beliefs, practices, and teachings of Freemasonry. Even though most of them are not aware of what is really going on, it does not keep them from being subject to the spiritual oppression that results in being associated with the Masons.

The belief of Freemasonry contradicts what the Bible says. The Masons are an organization that their main purpose is to provide a method of spiritual illumination and salvation that is completely apart and in opposition to what the Bible says.

Masons teach that good works will promise you salvation. As the degree of the Masons gets higher, the occult gets stronger. When they say someone is given Light, what it really means is that they are taught the principles of occultism. Again, many people involved in the Masons do not know the depth of occultism and satanism they are allowing to be a part of their life, but the negative results are the same.

Something is happening in the supernatural world as these words are spoken, and these oaths are being made. What is happening is that negative soul ties are being formed that will affect not only that person but continue on down the family line. These negative effects will go down from generation to generation.

But know this, God is there and the name of Jesus and the blood of Jesus can set us free from all the demonic strongholds.

We have to realize that there is a problem. We have to take action, and we have to renounce the rites, oaths, and ungodly beliefs of Freemasonry, calling upon Jesus to heal and deliver us. We have to cut off the enemy's access to us.

Know as you step out and pray, your body and mind will be healed. Relationships will be restored. Infirmities will leave. Depression will go. Breakthrough will come and the spirit of robbery will go.

The Lord wants us to be healed, set free and delivered. He no longer wants us to bear burdens that are not ours. He wants to break off all the affliction we have delt with due to the sins or our ancestors. We each have to repent and confess our own sin to receive the forgiveness of the Lord. Even though we are not responsible for our ancestors' sins, they still can affect us.

Ask the Holy Spirit to guide you through the prayer of repentance regarding Freemasonry. When you pray this prayer God will break off the curse of Freemasonry in your life, and in the life of your family. Know that as you receive your freedom, greater blessings will be released upon you by your heavenly Father.

Please see the prayer of freedom from Freemasonry in the next chapter.

CHAPTER 10 Prayer to be set free from Freemasonry

Prayer for Freedom from Freemasonry (This prayer model has been taken [and adapted] from Unmasking Freemasonry by S. Stevens; it is used with permission.) He recommends that the person who is seeking freedom, read the following prayer aloud. While this prayer is lengthy, the extra time is of little consequence to the benefit of assuring that all open gates are closed.

Father God, Creator of heaven and earth, I come to you in the name of Jesus Christ, your Son. I come as a sinner seeking forgiveness and cleansing from all sins committed against you and others made in your image. I honor my earthly father and mother and all of my flesh and blood ancestors, and also those of the spirit by adoption and godparents, but I utterly turn away from and renounce all their sins.

I forgive all my relatives and ancestors for passing on the effects of their sins to me and my children. I confess and renounce all of my own sins in this area as well. I renounce and rebuke Satan and every spiritual power of his which affects me and all members of my family, in the worthy name of Jesus.

I renounce and forsake all involvement in freemasonry or any other lodge or craft by my ancestors, my relatives, and by myself.

I renounce witchcraft, the principal spirit behind freemasonry, and I renounce Baphomet—the Spirit of Antichrist and the curse of the Luciferian doctrine. I renounce the idolatry, blasphemy, secrecy, and deception of Masonry at every level. I specifically renounce the insecurity, the love of position and power, the love of money, avarice and greed, and the pride which led my ancestors into Masonry. I renounce all the fears which held them in Masonry, especially the fear of death, the fear of men, and the fear of trusting, in the precious name of Jesus Christ.

I renounce every position held in the lodge by myself and any of my ancestors, including "Tyler," "Master," "Worshipful

Master" or any other. I renounce the calling of any man "Master," for Jesus Christ is my only master and Lord, and He forbids anyone else being called by that title.

I renounce the entrapping of others into Masonry and observing the helplessness of others during the rituals.

I renounce the effects of Masonry passed on to me through any female ancestor who felt distrusted and rejected by her husband as he entered and attended any lodge and refused to tell her of his secret activities.

I pray for all these favors in the blessed name of Jesus Christ, my Savior.

lst Degree I renounce the oaths taken and the curses involved in the 1st (or entered Apprentice) Degree, especially their effects on the throat and tongue.

I renounce the hoodwink (the blindfold) and its effects on the emotions and eyes, including all confusion, fear of the dark, fear of the light, and fear of sudden noises.

I renounce the secret word, BOAZ, and all it means. I renounce the mixing and mingling of truth and error, and the blasphemy of this degree of Masonry.

I renounce the noose around the neck, the fear of choking, and also every spirit causing asthma, hay fever, emphysema, or any other breathing difficulty.

I renounce the compass point, sword, or spear held against the breast, the fear of death by stabbing pain, and the fear of heart attack instilled from this degree.

I now pray for healing of the throat, vocal cords, nasal passages, sinuses, bronchial tubes, etc., for healing of the speech area, and the release of the Word of God to me and through me and all members of my family, in the name of Jesus Christ.

2nd Degree I renounce the oaths taken and the curses involved in the 2nd (or Fellow Craft) Degree of Masonry, especially the curses on the heart and chest.

I renounce the secret words JACHIN and SHIBBOLETH and all that these mean. I cut off the emotional hardness, apathy, indifference, unbelief, and deep anger, felt and experienced by me and all members of my family. I pray for the healing of my chest, lungs, and heart areas, and also for the healing of my emotions, and I ask that I be made sensitive to the Holy Spirit of God, in the name of Jesus Christ.

3rd Degree I renounce the oaths taken and the curses involved in the 3rd (or Master Mason) Degree, especially the curses on the stomach and womb area.

I renounce the secret words MAHA BONE, MACHABEN, MACHBINNA, and TUBAL CAIN, and all that they mean. I renounce the spirit of death from the blows to the head enacted as ritual murder, the fear of death and false martyrdom, the fear of violent gang attack, assault or rape, and the helplessness of this degree.

I renounce the falling into the coffin (or stretcher) involved in the ritual of murder.

I renounce the false resurrection of this degree, because only Jesus Christ is the Resurrection and the Life!

I also renounce the blasphemous kissing of the Bible on a witchcraft oath. I cut off all spirits of death, witchcraft, and deception, and in the name of Jesus Christ, I pray for the healing of (naming those that apply) my stomach, gall bladder, womb, liver, and any other organs of my body affected by masonry, and I ask for a release of compassion, understanding, and forgiveness for me and my family. I pray for all these favors in the blessed name of Jesus Christ.

Holy Royal Arch Degree I renounce and forsake the oaths taken and the curses and iniquities involved in the Holy Royal Arch Degree of Masonry, especially the oath regarding the removal of the head from the body and the exposing of the brains to the hot sun.

I renounce the Mark Lodge and the mark in the form of squares and angles which mark the person for life. I also reject the jewel, or talisman, which may have been made from this mark sign and worn at lodge meetings.

I renounce the false secret name of God, JAHBULON, and declare total rejection of all worship of false pagan gods, namely Bul or Baal and On or Osiris. I also renounce the password, AMMIRUHAMAH, and its occult meaning.

I renounce the false communion or eucharist taken in this degree, and all the mockery, skepticism, and unbelief about the redemptive work of Jesus Christ on the cross at Calvary. I repent of and cut off all these curses and their effects upon me and my family, and I command healing of the brain and the mind, in the name of Jesus Christ.

18th Degree I renounce the oaths taken and the curses involved in the 18th Degree of Masonry, the Most Wise Sovereign Knight of the Pelican and the Eagle and Sovereign Prince Rose Croix of Heredom.

I renounce and reject the Pelican witchcraft spirit, as well as the occult influence of the Rosicrucians and the Kabbala in this degree.

I renounce the claim that the death of Jesus Christ was a “dire calamity” and the deliberate mockery and twisting of the Christian doctrine of the Atonement.

I renounce the blasphemy and rejection of the deity of Jesus Christ and the secret words IGNE NATURA RENOVATURINTEGRA and its burning.

I renounce the mockery of the communion taken in this degree, including a biscuit, salt, and white wine, in the name of Jesus.

30th Degree I renounce the oaths taken and the curses involved in the 30th Degree of Masonry, the grand Knight Kadosh and Knight of the Black and White Eagle.

I renounce the password, STIBIUMALKABAR, and all it means, in the blessed name of Jesus.

31st Degree I renounce the oaths taken and the curses involved in the 31st Degree of Masonry, the Grand Inspector Inquisitor Commander.

I renounce all the gods and goddesses of Egypt which are honored in this degree, including Anubis with the ram's head, Osiris the sun god, Isis the sister and wife of Osiris, and also the moon goddess.

I renounce the Soul of Cheres, the false symbol of immorality, the Chamber of the Dead and the false teaching of reincarnation, in the name of Jesus.

32nd Degree I renounce the oaths taken and the curses involved in the 32nd Degree of Masonry, the Sublime Prince of the Royal Secret.

I renounce masonry's false trinitarian deity, AUM, and its parts: Brahma (the creator), Vishnu (the preserver) and Shiva (the destroyer).

I renounce the deity of AHURA-MAZDA, the claimed spirit or source of all light, and the worship with fire (which is an abomination to God), and drinking from a human skull, as done in some societal rites, in the name of Jesus Christ.

York Rite I renounce the oaths taken and the curses involved in the York Rite of freemasonry, including Mark Master, Past Master, Most Excellent Master, Royal Master, Select Master, Super Excellent Master, the Orders of the Red Cross, the Knights of Malta, and the Knights Templar degrees.

I renounce the secret words of JOPPA, KEBRAIOTH, and MAHERSHALAL-HASHBAZ.

I renounce the vows taken on a human skull, the crossed swords, and the curse and death wish of Judas, of having the head cut off and placed on top of a church spire.

I renounce the unholy communion and especially drinking from a human skull, as done in some societal rites, in the blessed name of Jesus Christ.

Shriners I renounce the oaths taken and the curses and penalties involved in the Ancient Arabic Order of Nobles of the Mystic Shrine.

I renounce the piercing of the eyeballs with a three-edged blade, the flaying of the feet, the madness, and the worship of the false god Allah, the god of our fathers.

I renounce the hoodwink, the mock hanging, the mock beheading, the mock drinking of the blood of the victim, the mock dog urinating on the initiate, and the offering of urine as a commemoration, in the blessed name of Jesus Christ.

33rd Degree I renounce the oaths taken and the curses involved in the 33rd Degree of Masonry, the Grand Sovereign Inspector General.

I renounce and forsake the declaration that Lucifer is God.

I renounce the cable-tow around the neck.

I renounce the death wish—that the wine drunk from a human skull should turn to poison—and the skeleton, whose cold arms are solicited if the oath of this degree is violated.

I renounce the three infamous assassins of their Grand Master, law, property, and religion, and the greed and witchcraft involved in the attempt to manipulate and control the rest of mankind, in the blessed name of Jesus Christ.

All Other Degrees I renounce all the other oaths taken, the rituals of every other degree, and the curses therein involved.

I renounce all other lodges and secret societies, such as Prince Hall Freemasonry, Mormonism, The Order of Amaranth, Oddfellows, the Buffalos, Druids, Foresters, Orange, Elks, Moose and Eagles Lodges, the Ku Klux Klan, The Grange, the Woodmen of the World, Rider of the Red Robe, the Knights of Pythias, the Mystic Order of the Veiled Prophets of the Enchanted Realm, the women's Orders of the Eastern Star and of the White Shrine of Jerusalem, the girls' Order of the Daughters of the Eastern Star, the International Orders of Job's Daughters and of Rainbow Girls, and the boy's Order of DeMolay, and their effects upon me and all members of my family, in the precious name of Jesus Christ.

I renounce the ancient pagan teaching and symbolism of the First Tracing Board, the Second Tracing Board, and the Third Tracing Board, as used in the rituals of the Blue Lodge.

I renounce the pagan ritual of the "Point with a Circle" with all its bondages and phallus (penis) worship.

I renounce the occult mysticism of the black and white mosaic checkered floor, with the tessellated (or adorned) pagan symbolism and bondages.

I renounce and utterly forsake the Great Architect of the Universe, who is revealed in the higher degrees as Lucifer, and his false claim to be the universal fatherhood of God.

I also renounce the false claim that Lucifer is the Morning Star and Shining One, and I declare that Jesus Christ alone is the Bright and Morning Star spoken of in Revelation 22:16.

I renounce the All-Seeing Third Eye of freemasonry or Horus in the forehead and its pagan and occult symbolism.

I renounce all false communions, all mockery of the redemptive work of Jesus Christ on the cross at Calvary, all unbelief, confusion, and depression, and all worship of Lucifer as God.

I renounce and forsake the lie of freemasonry—that man is not sinful, just imperfect, and so can redeem himself through good works.

I rejoice that the Bible declares that I cannot do a single thing to earn my salvation, and that I can only be saved by grace through faith in Jesus Christ and what He accomplished on the Cross at Calvary.

I renounce all fear of insanity, anguish, death wishes, suicide, and death in the name of Jesus Christ. Death was conquered by Jesus Christ, and He alone holds the keys of death and health, and

I rejoice that He holds my life in His hands even now. He came to give me life abundantly and eternally, and I believe in His promises.

I renounce all anger, hatred, murderous thoughts, revenge, retaliation, spiritual apathy, false religion, and unbelief, especially unbelief in the Holy Bible as God's Word, and all occasions of compromising God's Word.

I renounce all spiritual searching into false religions and all my striving to please God, who already knows and loves me eternally. I rest in the knowledge that I have found my Lord and Savior, Jesus Christ, and that I am no more "lost" to Him—He has found me.

I will burn all objects in my possession which connect me with all lodges and occult organizations, including masonry, and witchcraft, their regalia, aprons, books of rituals, rings, and other apparel and jewelry.

I renounce the effects these (or other objects of masonry, such as the compass, the square, the noose, or the blindfold) have had upon me or any members of my family, in Jesus' blessed name.

Holy Spirit, I ask that you show me anything else I need to do or from which I need to pray, so that I and all members of my family may be totally free from the consequences of the sins of masonry, witchcraft, and paganism—and from any and all things unrighteous. Now, Father God, I ask humbly for the blood of Jesus Christ, your Son, to cleanse me from all these sins of which I have confessed and renounced, to cleanse my spirit, my soul, my mind, my emotions, and every part of my body which has been affected by these sins, in Jesus' holy name!

I renounce every evil spirit associated with masonry, witchcraft, and all other sins, and I command—in the name of Jesus Christ—for Satan and every evil spirit to be bound and to leave me now, touching or harming no one, and that they go to the place appointed by the Lord Jesus, never again to return to me or any member of my family. I call on the name of the Lord Jesus alone to be delivered of these spirits, in accordance with the many promises mentioned in the Bible. I ask to be delivered of every spirit of sickness, infirmity, curse, affliction, addiction, disease, or allergy associated with these sins of which I have confessed and renounced.

I surrender to God's Holy Spirit—and to no other spirit—all the places in my life where these sins have been. I ask you, Lord, to baptize me in your Holy Spirit now, according to the promises of your Word. I take to myself the whole armor of God in accordance with Ephesians chapter six and rejoice in its protection as Jesus surrounds me and fills me with His Holy Spirit.

I enthrone you, Lord Jesus, within my heart, for you are my Lord and my Savior, the source of eternal life. Thank you, Father God, for your mercy, your forgiveness, and your life, in the name of Jesus Christ I pray. Amen. (Note: Those who have actually been involved in the various degrees of freemasonry are encouraged to symbolically do the following, as they read the prayer above.)

1. Symbolically remove the blindfold (hoodwink) and give it to the Lord for disposal.
2. In the same way, symbolically remove the veil of mourning.
3. Symbolically cut and remove the noose from around the neck; gather it up with the cable-tow running down the body and give it all to the Lord for His disposal.
4. Renounce the false freemasonry marriage covenant, removing from the 4th finger of the right hand the ring of this false marriage covenant and giving it to the Lord to dispose of.
5. Symbolically remove the chains and bondages of freemasonry from your body.

6. Symbolically remove all freemasonry regalia and armor, especially the apron.
7. Symbolically remove the ball and chain from the ankles.
8. Repent of and seek forgiveness for having walked on unholy ground, including freemasonry lodges and temples.
9. Proclaim that Satan and his demons no longer have any legal right to mislead and manipulate you.

I pray as you read this prayer and pray it over yourself that it brings you great freedom for yourself and your family.

Be sure that you pray the prayer out loud. You can pray it several times. Keep praying it until you feel you are free.

CHAPTER 11 Summary

I know there is a lot more information regarding Freemasonry. I know that I only touch the surface. However, my prayer is that what I said will open your eyes to desire to see the truth and to know the truth and know that the truth will set you free.

I recommend if you or your family member are, or were, in the Masons, and you still after reading this book are not convinced that Freemasonry is demonic, and that it can destroy your life and your family's life, please take some time and spend it with the Lord. Ask Him to open your eyes to see the truth.

Before I became a Christian, I really enjoyed Halloween. One Sunday after I had gotten saved, our pastor taught on the dangers of Halloween. I sat in the service thinking this is crazy there is nothing wrong with Halloween or going trick-or-treating. I ignored what my pastor had said, and I took my two small children trick-or-treating.

The Lord, begin to open my eyes to see all the demonic that really happened on Halloween night. I was scared to death that night. I told God that night, I said Lord if you keep me and my babies safe, and let us get home safe, I will never participate in Halloween again.

So, if you ask God to show you the truth about Freemasonry He will, just like He showed me the truth about Halloween.

The devil has a legal right to make us sick, to torment us as long as we are still connected with the demonic stronghold that the Masons have on us. We have to cut it off and cast it away from us.

The Bible is not in agreement with us being in the Masons. The Bible is clear that there is only one God. That God is the God we serve. The trinity God the Father, Jesus the Son, and the Holy Spirit. We should never serve any other God.

The Masons have their own Bible it is called a Masonic Bible. It is a collection of texts that the Freemasonry use. It includes religious texts that fit the teachings and beliefs of Freemasonry. These texts come from different religions. It is not one book; it has many texts. All these texts are held in high regard by Freemasons.

The Masonic Bible has its own distinct history and origin. This book was written so the Masons would have their own version of the Bible. This book has Masonic symbols and messages in its pages.

The text in this book has been modified from that of the standard Bible. It has excerpts from writings by different Masons. It also has engravings depicting several scenes from Masonic rituals and ceremonies.

This book contains rituals, symbols, and allegories unique to freemasonry. This book has teachings in it from religions such as Buddhism, and Hinduism. In this book they do not refer to God but to the Grand Architect of the Universe.

In this book they focus on their own personal growth instead of growing and maturing in the Lord Jesus Christ.

So, again I ask that you really pray and seek God regarding the Masons if you are thinking of joining. My believe is that this is not a Christian organization. It has hidden agenda, and my belief is that if you join this organization, it can and will open doors for the demonic not only in your life but in your family's life as well.

Ask yourself what does Freemasonry teach? Do they teach God and salvation? Is what they teach go against what the Bible says. For example, the Bible says there is only one God. Freemasonry omits God and Jesus, and they worship the Grand Architect of the Universe. The Masons core teachings contradict the Bible.

Freemasonry calls God "The Great Architect of the Universe." This is their name for God. Again, when they pray, they do not pray in the name of Jesus.

Again, Freemasonry is by invitation only. Members pledge secrecy to the society. They have secret words, pledges, rituals, vows, and phrases. They speak secret curses on themselves, and their families if they break their vows.

Members go through a progressive revelation or indoctrination, level by level.

Wikipedia says, in the course of three degrees, new Masons will promise to keep the secrets of their degree from lower degrees and outsiders, and to support a fellow Mason in distress.

Freemasonry is a secret society, and it deliberately conceals the truth not only to outsiders but to those in the lower degrees and other members outside of the leadership.

At the highest levels of Freemasonry, those members know that they are actually serving and worshipping Satan himself.

Freemasonry is an open door for many people to pick up demons. A lot of people have demons because of freemasonry, or someone in their family ancestral line being in the Masons. Like other demonic problems, demons and their problems, lusts, etc. can be passed down family lines.

Exodus 34:7 says, by no means clearing the guilty, visiting the iniquity of the fathers upon the children and the children's children to the third and the fourth generation.

Contact Information

Contact us through the contact form on our website:

thomasvelez.com

To order more books by Fay Velez:

- The Power of Prayer that brings Healings & Miracles
- Spirits that keep us bound
- Powerful Nuggets from the Lord
- Going from ungodly to Godly
- Spirits that try to stay Hidden
- Hearing the Voice of God Daily
- Spirits that Destroy Churches & Businesses
- Unlocking the Prophetic in us
- The Damage of Freemasonry

- Get Free Stay Free (Thomas & Fay Velez)

To order more books by Thomas Velez:

- Personal Spiritual Warfare
- Army of the Lord Arising

- Understanding the Book of Revelation
- Antichrist Invades the Earth
- God saved My Life 29 Times

Order online from websites:

thomasvelez.com

and also at:

Amazon.com

Made in the USA
Columbia, SC
22 April 2024